ST. THOMAS MORE AT THE MILLENNIUM

March 2001

Ray and Peg,

My gratitude for your kindness, friendship and love of Thomas More. 'Merrily in Christ'!

Bob Gray
Naples

ST. THOMAS MORE AT THE MILLENNIUM

By

C. ROBERT WRAY

ISBN: 0-75960-431-2

This book is printed on acid free paper.

1stBooks - rev. 01/26/01

I wish to acknowledge

My wife, Paula, for loyalty and understanding; our two strong daughters, Kathanne and Maura, and their loving families, Bob, Chesleigh and Julia; Jack, Tierney and Patrick. And to Sheila! Betty Hourihan and Professor Charles Rice for advice and encouragement. Jack Costello; Connie McManmon;. Fr. Thomas McAvoy, C.S.C., mentor and historian; Monsignors who love the martyr, EugeneV. Clark in New York City and Anthony Stark in Wimbledon, London; Fr. Alan Hopes who lovingly oversees "The Church of the Most Holy Redeemer and St. Thomas More" in Chelsea, London; numerous librarians in Chelsea, West Falmouth on Cape Cod; Naples, Florida. Beth Mariner for her help and especially Joanne Laibinis for her caring effort.

Here's to Chris!

St. Thomas More's Life

1478	Birth
1494	Leaves Oxford to study law
1496	Enters Lincoln's Inn, law college
1499	Friendship with Erasmus
1504	Marries Jane Colt... *(Margaret, Elizabeth, Cecily, John)*
1509	Henry VIII succeeds father as King
1510-1518	Undersheriff of London
1511	Jane More dies; marries Alice Middleton
1516	<u>Utopia</u>
1518	In the service of the King
1521	Knighted ("Sir" Thomas More)
1523-4	Speaker, House of Commons; Defender of Henry VIII vs. Luther; Chancellor, Royal Duchy of Lancaster
1529	Lord Chancellor

1532	Resigns as Lord Chancellor
1534	Imprisoned for refusing oath to Act of Succession
1535	Trial and conviction of treason; beheaded (July 6)
1886	Beatified by Pope Leo XIII
1935	Canonized ("Saint") by Pope Pius XI
2000	Proclaimed "Patron Saint of Politicians" by Pope John Paul II

I

"Timeless St. Thomas More, a man for all seasons, is stirring again, his words echoing from the banks of the Thames River to the banks of the Potomac and Tiber Rivers."

Timeless St. Thomas More, a man for all seasons, is stirring again, his words echoing from the banks of the Thames River to the banks of the Potomac River. In England Archbishop of Canterbury George Carey has declared the Anglican Church will honor Thomas More in the "String of Pearls Millennium Festival". In America Special Prosecutor Kenneth Starr, Congressman Henry J. Hyde and other players in the Impeachment and Trial of President William J. Clinton made frequent reference to Thomas More's name. And, in Rome, Pope John Paul II prepared to proclaim on November 5, 2000 Saint Thomas More the "Patron of Statesmen and Politicians."

In sixteenth century England Thomas More served as King Henry VIII's long time advisor, being elevated to Lord Chancellor in 1529. Widely respected as a public servant, author, and Christian humanist, More was wholly committed to the unity of what he called "Christ's known Catholic Church", which led to his resignation and silent opposition when the King decided to divorce his Queen, marry Anne Boleyn, and create the Anglican Church, initiating the English Reformation. Imprisoned in the Tower of London, tried for treason and executed in 1535, Thomas More left a bright example of martyrdom, which led to his canonization as a saint by the Roman Catholic Church in the twentieth century.

In 1936, a year after More's canonization, English philosopher Gilbert Keith Chesterton alerted us that the newest Saint was to be even more important in decades ahead. His words deserve attention, as he could not have foreseen the impeachment and trial of an American President nor the interest of the Anglican Church, begun by Henry VIII, in a man, Thomas More, who accepted death rather than approve the dismantlement of the Catholic Church. It is interesting that the Anglican Church has 'adopted' him and included a "Thomas More Trail of the

Thames" as a major part of the Millennium Festival. In January of 2000 More's cell room in the Bell Tower of the Tower of London was opened for the first time to the public. Anglican Canon Colin Fletcher spoke of the experience of being in the cell, where More spent the last fifteen months of his life, as "a wonderfully evocative place...very moving...a lonely place." The Thomas More Trail also includes his birthplace on Milk Street, London in 1478; Lambeth Palace, closed to visitors since 1951, where nine year old Thomas More served as a page to the Archbishop of Canterbury; possibly to Chelsea Old Church with its More Chapel and Vault and the martyr's statue outside overlooking the embankment along the Thames; to the Chapel Royal of St. Peter ad Vincula (in chains) on the Tower of London grounds where More's body was buried in 1535; and to nearby Tower Hill where he was beheaded. Serious pilgrims will journey to Canterbury, whose Cathedral for centuries has been a renowned pilgrimage site as the place Thomas a' Beckett was assassinated, and visit St. Dunstan's Anglican Church. The church holds a small lead casket containing the head of Thomas More in the Vault of the Roper family into which his eldest daughter, Margaret, married.

Across the Atlantic the name of Thomas More was used frequently by members of the House of Representatives, witnesses and staff throughout the impeachment and trial of the President. Argument over the meaning of passages and words arose between Democrats and Republicans, each side anxious to align the martyr's mystique behind their cause. However, none of the several quotations on topics such as perjury, conscience and sanctity of an oath were ever uttered by More. The references used by congressional leaders, prosecutors and staff came from Robert Bolt, author of the splendid play "A Man for All Seasons". Bolt, neither a Christian nor a Catholic, admitted to struggling with the inner person of his subject. His play, successful and memorable as a work of art, was neither historically nor theologically accurate. Those seeking to remove the President from the White House took an easy path by quoting Bolt, leading observers to wonder if a copy of Bolt's work was passed around the House Judiciary Committee to the Committee counsel and to the Special Prosecutor. Thomas More's own words would have conveyed a deeper, more theological meaning, perhaps why they were not employed. If the More references were to impress a national audience, they drew little attention. The media, swarming over the Impeachment hearings in the

House of Representatives and the subsequent 1999 Trial in the United States Senate, all but ignored the Thomas More references from the proceedings. An interested party to these absorbing and historic events did, however. On Sunday, January 31, 1999 William Jefferson Clinton purchased a copy of the recent biography The Life of Thomas More by Peter Ackroyd. In the coming pages we will endeavor to discover Thomas More, seeking the inner man that has alluded many of those now writing about him or elevating his name along both the Thames and the Atlantic.

Another politician, Francesco Cossica, former President of Italy, urged the Vatican to honor Thomas More at the Jubilee for World Parliamentarians, Statesmen and Politicians meeting in Rome in November, 2000. Adopting this idea, Cardinal Paul Poupard observed that politics "Is a field for the greatest kind of charity. We need a new generation of politicians who are convinced of that, and the witness of Thomas More will offer them an example to follow." The Pope subsequently decreed More as the "Patron of Statesmen and Politicians."

II

"The person of the greatest virtue this kingdom ever had."

Jonathan Swift

Born on Milk Street in London in February 1478, young Thomas More entered a respected and successful family. His father, John More, later to become Chief Justice of King's Bench, England's highest court, provided Thomas with entree to the Royal Court. His life and that of future King Henry VIII, became entwined late in the fifteenth century. More never took advantage of this relationship. He treated the younger Henry before and after his ascension to Kingship as a member of the highest class, the person chosen by God to rule England. More believed monarchy was divinely established for reasons none but God could know. It was the duty of the citizens of the state to respect and obey. He took this view to the scaffold on Tower Hill where under final orders from Henry VIII, More died on July 6, 1535. Prophetic of this was an event years earlier, following a social visit to the More household by the King. William Roper reported More's words after the monarch left: "If my head could win him a castle in France, it should not fail to go." Contrary to the words of many authors and More loyalists, Thomas More viewed the King as his 'lord', never his 'friend'. In the final public statement More proudly declared he remained until the end of his life "the King's loyal servant."

Thomas More was educated at St. Anthony's School in London and in the household of the Archbishop of Canterbury and Lord Chancellor, John Morton. In his early teens he was sent to Oxford University's Canterbury Hall, an arrangement by Cardinal Morton who observed the youth to be a "merry boy" who would become "a marvelous man." Religious devotion and intellectual awareness were strengths More exhibited throughout all his life. The Cardinal used the word "merry" to describe More and this word became a fixture in the young man's writing and speech. To "meet merrily in heaven" was the phrase he sincerely gave to friend and enemy alike, even wishing it to the nineteen judges who voted for his guilt and execution in Westminster Hall. Possessing a witty nature, he twitted with words and ideas without ever being hurtful. This jesting approach surfaced in many of his writings and in relationships with family and friends.

About 1494 More entered London's New Inn as a student. His father planned a law career for his only son, withdrawing him early from Oxford to ensure he did not deepen his enthusiasm for humanism and the New Learning of the Renaissance. By this time Thomas had a strong knowledge of French, Latin, mathematics, and history. He also had mastery of the flute and viol. He studied Greek later to read and understand the Church fathers. Upon entering Lincoln's Inn he progressed rapidly in his legal education, being called to the bar at an early age. More found time to pursue writing, producing verse and comedies in both English and Latin while lecturing and teaching, especially focusing on St. Augustine's City of God. From his days at St. Anthony's and Oxford, More had many intellectual friends and companions. These included England's finest young humanist thinkers and scholars from whom he received stimuli to advance his learning and deepen his faith. A deep and lasting friendship began with Erasmus whom he met on his first visit to England. Their correspondence and exchange of intimate views continued for many years. After his execution Erasmus lamented his friend as one "whose soul was more pure than any snow, whose genius was such that England never had - yea, and never shall have again, mother of good wits though England be."

As the sixteenth century began More was a lawyer, an author, a highly respected Christian humanist thinker. For four years during his legal studies he lived like a Carthusian monk whose order's London Charterhouse was where he daily attended Mass, prayed and practiced his faith. Close to becoming a Carthusian or Franciscan monk, he wore a hairshirt of rough texture and kept a small flagon for self mortification. He used these until the day before his death when he turned them over to his daughter Margaret's maid. When these practices began, More was living a monk's lifestyle described by Erasmus as including "vigils, fasts, and prayers, and similar austerities." In 1503 More came to the decision that his vocation was not for the priesthood. Many explanations have been offered - disgust with church corruption, ambition for advancement in politics and law, rejection of celibacy, an only son's duty to carry out his father's wish and the family name. His own words to Erasmus tell us he rejected the priesthood and chose to marry because "being unable to master the desire for a wife, he decided to be a chaste husband rather than a priest impure."

III

"The things, good Lord, that I pray for,

Give me the grace to labor for."

Thomas More's final written prayer.

In 1504 Thomas More married Jane Colt, the eldest daughter of a well known family. They set up house in the Barge, Bucklesbury in London. Elected to the House of Commons in Parliament he began a very successful legal and political career leading to his becoming Lord Chancellor in 1529. Erasmus visited and stayed with the Mores on at least two occasions, writing his famous Praise of Folly there, the title in Latin being *"Moriae Encomium"*, a play on the name of Thomas More to whom the famous work was dedicated. In the summer of 1511 Jane More died, probably in childbirth. Thomas More was left with four children, three daughters and a son, the youngest. He soon married again, obtaining a dispensation to wed a widow seven years his senior, Alice Middleton, "without banns asking" to expedite the marriage. Her first husband, John Middleton, had been a merchant of the *Staple of Calais*, signifying considerable assets and influence. Alice inherited considerable wealth and property. Her one living daughter, also an Alice, entered the More household as a full family member, later marrying into English nobility and becoming a direct forebearer of present day Queen Elizabeth II.

Alice More never wholly appreciated her second husband's jestful ways but, according to her biographer, Ruth Norrington, gave as good as she got. She ran the household energetically, assisting in it becoming an ever important and vital site as its Master's prominence and influence increased in the coming years. It also became the location of the More form of Academy for the education of the children and wards. She was only partially successful in improving her second husband's habits. More was careless and untidy in dress and attire. His new wife was able to ensure his appearance improved. However, even though she sought the assistance of the family's parish priest, she was unable to stop her husband wearing the hairshirt she so loathed. Thomas More began to use his oldest daughter, Margaret called Meg, to clean and care for the shirt. He never spoke of this practice of self mortification and few knew of it.

Lady Alice, Meg, and, later, Anne Cresacre, a young ward, who spied the undergarment at lunch on a hot summer day and her laughter made More take steps never to have it viewed that way again. Anne later married his only son, John More.

IV

"To warn my children to avoid the precipices of pride and haughtiness, and to walk in the pleasant meadows of modesty, not to be dazzled at the site of gold; not to lament that they do not possess what they erroneously admire in others, not to think more of themselves for gaudy trappings, nor less for the want of them, neither to deform the beauty that nature has given by neglect, nor to try to heighten it by artifice, to put virtue in the first place, learning in the second, and in their studies to esteem most whatever may teach them piety toward God, charity to all, and Christian humility in themselves."

Thomas More to his children's tutor.

In the More household there were daily prayers, evening readings from the Psalms and recitations from the Beatitudes. At dinner each night one of the children read a passage from Scripture with commentary and discussion following. All adults and children played musical instruments with evening song and music ensuring a merry and pious atmosphere, though More had a poor singing voice.

Thomas More was one of his era's foremost educators. His 'home school curriculum' included French, Latin, science, astrology, history, literature, and religion as main subjects. His children and wards were highly learned and daughter Margaret was among Europe's most educated and cultured women. Henry VIII's illegitimate son, the Duke of Richmond, was educated by tutors who took their guidelines from Thomas More. More also used tutors to educate his children and wards. His letters to the tutors while he was away on diplomatic mission or at the Royal Court deserve reading today. His philosophy and values have enduring qualities. He also saw men and women having the same nature "and equally suited for learning, for study and erudition and ultimately for the final goal, and fruit of these endeavors, a good conscience." More knew his advocacy of women's learning would be under some attack but he stressed "the reward of wisdom is too solid to be lost like riches or to decay like beauty, since it depends on the intimate conscience of what is right, not on the talk of men, then which nothing is more foolish or mischievous." In support of his view for the cultivation of female learning he cited the opinions of the ancients and wrote how both St. Jerome and St. Augustine exhorted matrons and virgins to study, even having " diligently explained the abstruse meaning of Holy Scriptures, and wrote for tender girls letters replete with so much erudition, that nowadays old men, who call themselves professors of sacred science, can scarcely read them correctly, no less understand them."

The schools at More's houses in London and from 1525 in Chelsea at what he called "the greatest house" on his 34 acre estate, included his four children born from 1505 to 1509 - Margaret, Elizabeth, Cecily and John; numerous wards some of whom married his children and all of whom were treated by him as members of his family; and relatives including grandchildren of whom there would be eleven at his death. Erasmus referred to Thomas More's school as "Plato's Academy...come to life again" with an emphasis on piety and the knowledge and practice of the Christian faith.

More made a strong work ethic a constant ingredient in the education of his children and wards. Each had a daily task to perform, developing responsibility and an obligation to contribute to the common good. Charity to others, especially the less fortunate, was an essential element in developing progress toward virtue and Christian piety. His own example, though done quietly, was significant in educating his extended family. More maintained and financed an alms house for the poor, the homeless, the ill, the aged. He personally walked the streets of London and, later, Chelsea to dispense his own coins and gifts to the needy. Regularly he sought word of people in distress and provided money, food, supplies and his own counsel as each case required. Thomas More, living at the time of the beginnings of the Reformation in all of Europe and in England in particular, hated heresy but never the heretic. Recent critics of his attacks on heretics have not always explored his actions and reasons. His own son-in-law, William Roper, after marrying Margaret, his most beloved daughter, became a zealous Protestant Reformer. Called before Archbishop of Canterbury Wolsey, Roper was released but persisted in his views. Thomas More despaired, his own counsel and warnings going unheeded. He knew he had to turn his son-in-law in to the ecclesiastical court, and was close to doing so, when Will Roper recanted, becoming a

Catholic again. He also became forever indebted to his father-in-law, reverently serving him as an assistant and companion. The importance of Roper readopting Catholicism and his turning away from Lutheranism was that it had to have a strong influence on Thomas More, who continued ever hopeful of similar conversions as he sought to stem the spread of heresy but to save the heretic.

V

"The best friend the poor ever had."

Shakespeare on Thomas More

Stories of More's concern for the less fortunate are many. Two are useful here. In 1529 he was away with the Court in Woodstock when a disastrous fire destroyed the barns on his Chelsea estate where he allowed poorer neighbors to store grain with his own crops. Alice More was distraught in her letter to him. He answered his wife not to be concerned for their loss but to ensure that none of the laborers who worked for them were released. And, he would aid his poor neighbors first for "I should not leave myself a spoon there, shall be so poor neighbor of mine bear no loss by any chance happened in my house." His instinctive sense was to protect others in need before being concerned for his personal loss. Another illustration of his regard for the needy was witnessed on the many feast days and celebrations of the time when More always invited the less fortunate and needy from all streets, places and circumstances to join his table where he and his family hosted them. He never included nobility or the more affluent on such occasions.

More served the people of London, some 50,000 in the early 1500's. Elected Under Sheriff in 1507, he became the legal protector of the inhabitants and he knew this meant inevitable disagreements with King and Court. When Henry VIII succeeded his father in 1509 he pressured More, whom he deeply respected and admired, to join the court. But More resisted, unwilling to desert his role serving his city's fellow commoners. After being twice sent abroad on diplomatic and trade missions by the King, More was drawn in to royal service in 1516, becoming a member of both the Privy Council and the Star Chamber, two of the most powerful decision making bodies in the realm. By 1518 Thomas More was wholly in service to the King. Thus ended his daily work for the people of London but his charity and service to the neediest never ceased. Years later at the end of the 16th century, William Shakespeare called Thomas More "the best friend the poor ever had", echoing Erasmus' accolade that his friend was "the patron of all in need." This value of service to charity and service to others was integral to education in the More household, too, and every person had to perform service to others. Family members replaced him when he was absent to ensure the work continued. As the world enters a new millennium the life and example of Thomas More have much to instruct us.

VI

"They had no lawyers among them, for they consider them as a sort of people whose profession it is to disguise matters."

Thomas More, Utopia

Writing was a life long passion for Thomas More, attested to by the volumes constituting his 'complete works' today. Among his earliest works were The Life of Picodella Mirodola, the young Christian humanist who died at 31; the translation of the second century satirist Lucian from Greek into Latin; and in 1515-1516 Utopia, written in Latin, an immediate and lasting favorite of continental humanists. Meaning "not place", Utopia in two books questioned the era's assumptions and beliefs on numerous matters. The mythical non-Christian island community and its society reflected aspects of Plato's Republic. In dialogue form, common to the age, More raised provocative questions on topics ranging through economic, social, political, and religious values.

His own views are never clearly revealed but Utopia, not translated into English until 1551, well after More's death, provoked its intelligent readers and made its author a celebrity of the age's humanists. The History of Richard III in Latin and English was popular in Tudor England for its view of the fifteenth century English monarch, whose defeat and death brought the Tudor dynasty to power, as monster, hypocrite and murderer. Shakespeare adopted this very view in his 1594 play. More also published a compilation of his numerous pithy epigrams, poetry and preces. Later, the spread of the Protestant Reformation during his court service made More turn to defense of Christian unity and to defense of King Henry. An emphasis in most of his writings was on religion, the religious life, and on prayer. His letters also testify to the constant priority these themes had in his daily life.

In 1518 Erasmus sent More a copy of the ninety-five theses Martin Luther had made public in Wittenberg, Germany the previous year. The event triggered the Protestant Reformation and the life of Thomas More would never be the same again. Luther's attack on the Catholic Church and its doctrines, such as the seven sacraments, brought Henry VIII into the fray. He wrote a treatise, Assertion of the Seven Sacraments. This defended Catholic teachings and beliefs and attacked Luther and his new ideas. More, now ever at the King's side, edited and helped publish the work but did not write it. Ironically, he urged Henry to "subdue his enthusiasm for papal supremacy" expressed in the work. But Henry VIII told Thomas More that he firmly believed in this doctrine and that "we shall set forth (the Papacy's) authority to the uttermost." He added that he believed that we "receive from that See our crown Imperial." Clearly in 1521 Henry firmly held the belief that papal supremacy was an absolute. Advisor and secretary to the King, Thomas More began to study this strong view. It was not something he had explored before. His older cleric friend and sometime advisor, Bishop John Fisher, held the same view and deepened More's understanding and eventual firm acceptance of papal supremacy. More and Fisher would go to their deaths weeks apart in 1535 holding firmly to the doctrine while Henry would abandon it once it no longer served his needs. But, in 1521, Henry was named "The Defender of the Faith" by Pope Leo X, a title English monarchs still use.

Henry's attack on Luther and his doctrines led to the German ex-priest savaging the English monarch in a viscous and scatological response. Thomas More was ordered to reply to Luther in 1523 and did so in Responsio ad Lutherum, continuing the reformer's style and approach while defending King and Catholic Church. More's words and deeds have been criticized by some modern biographers. Even Anne Murphy explains in her scholarly and supportive Thomas More in the "Great Christian Thinkers" series. She tells us: "More's deepest reasons for persecuting heretics were theological and religious: heresy was a kind of treason of the soul, and endangered the eternal salvation of other Christians." As More saw it, to put the soul of another person in jeopardy resembled cutting that person off from God for all eternity. Such an action, he thought, deserved the death penalty, and with it took the forlorn hope that it might produce a last minute recantation. Murphy confesses that in her opinion "his fierce intolerance towards heretics, and the part he played in execution, cannot be defended...It remains distressing that in this matter More was a man of his time, not a man for all seasons."

VII

"...heretics, I hate the view of theirs and not their persons."

Thomas More

The 1520's saw heresy take center stage in England. Efforts to ban books, prevent 'reform' ideas from arriving from the continent, threaten those who refused to obey, all failed to reverse its spread. Under Cardinal Wolsey's joint tenure as Archbishop of Canterbury and Lord Chancellor, no heretics were executed. Thomas More succeeded Wolsey, disgraced by failure to get the See of Rome's approval for the annulment of Henry's marriage to Queen Catherine, and was devoted to ceasing the spread of heresy and to preserving the unity of 'Christ's known Catholic Church.' His Confutation of Tynsdale's Answer in essay form defended his view of life and religion and attacked William Tynsdale, the leading writer for Lutheranism in English. The heart of More's thesis against Tynsdale and Lutheranism is presented by Louis F. Martz in Thomas More: The Search for the Inner Man. Martz writes that More's Augustinian view of man and religion was " a view that sees, not a church of 'elects' who cannot fall to damnation, however they may slip, but a church of fallen people, any one of whom has yet available the hope of redemption." The Lutheran view of "justification by faith alone" was confronted by More who affirmed that man earns salvation by his own good works and obedience to Christ's Church along with the grace of God. Faith, without good works, was not enough to gain heaven in this Catholic view of salvation.

During the three year period of More's Lord Chancellorship, heresy and the "reform" movement grew. More's fury in his writings continued what had started in the early 1520's between Luther and Henry VIII. Luther's words in 1522 against the King turned the language obscene. Martz holds that More's duty was thereafter to "bespatter Luther with the same Luther had hurled at Henry only more of it, if possible." But Martz denies this represents the 'inner man' of More. He was writing propaganda, supporting a cause as St. Augustine had "in his polemics against the Pelagions and the Manicheans..." More believed that as to "heretics, I hate the view of theirs and not their persons."

Some six heretics were burned during More's tenure as Lord Chancellor, three of whom he investigated and turned over to religious authority for trial only when convinced each was unrepentant and a threat, in his own words, "to do many folk much harm." This was his duty under the law, as it had been when he, years before, contemplated turning over his son-in-law, Will Roper, for his heretical views. Executions after Thomas More's era greatly increased. Several hundred died this way under Thomas Cromwell from 1535-1546. A ruthless age, 16th century English public execution, according to Martz and others, makes More's role pale in comparison to that of others. As the English Reformation More tried to prevent came into full bloom, both sides proved violent and cruel.

The Thomas More life trail was full of irony. He was abroad when Wolsey was removed by the King and was neither empowered nor enthused when Henry made him Lord Chancellor in 1529. The Parliament that began that year would last for eight years, go down in history as "the Reformation Parliament" and cooperate with the Crown to both end the unity of Christendom and change the structure of England forever. Lutheranism and 'reform' thinking and thinkers were represented in the House of Commons, in the House of Lords, in the countryside and in the Court. More was the third layman to serve as Lord Chancellor, two others having served brief fifteenth century terms. Beginning with More's elevation, the office was never again combined with that of Archbishop of Canterbury whose power would also diminish as Henry and subsequent monarchs became the head of the Church of England.

Loyal to Henry, More took on his new duties with conviction. The emerging issue was the King's "great matter", of annuling his marriage to Queen Catherine. Cardinal Wolsey had fallen mainly for failing to convince Papal emissary Cardinal Campeggio to declare the marriage invalid. Campeggio referred the issue back to Rome for final decision. Catherine had been wedded for dynastic reasons to Henry's older brother, Arthur, who died in 1502, six months after the unconsummated marriage. To continue the English and Spanish alliance, Prince Henry at age 16 married Catherine, his former sister-in-law, only after all sides, including the Roman See, agreed to the union's validity. By the mid 1520's Henry was restless, anxious to have a legitimate male heir, and tired of his older, aging wife. They had one living daughter, Mary. Catherine had had other pregnancies, even giving birth to a son, christened Henry, who only lived for fifty-seven days. In late 1527, Henry instigated a private talk with Thomas More asking his position on the validity of his marriage to Queen Catherine. More contemplated the matter and responded to the King that in his judgement the marriage was valid. Henry ordered him to study the issue further and to discuss it with Wolsey. Henry had found the biblical saying in Leviticus which said "Thou shall not uncover the nakedness of thy brother's wife...If a man takes his brother's wife...they shall be childless." Additionally, in 1526 Anne Boleyn appeared at court and it was not long before Henry was pursuing her with gifts and attention. Her sister had earlier been the King's mistress. The "great matter", as it came to be known, of Henry's annulment would be a dominant topic for the next six years. During this time Thomas More would neither alter nor modify his judgment that the marriage was valid, nor would he reveal his view and his response to the King to anyone.

During the 1520's Thomas More began to realize financial benefit from his service to King and Court. Cardinal Wolsey and the Duke of Norfolk, influential in court life and a More admirer, interceded with the King to improve his salary and benefits. In 1521 he was appointed Under-Treasurer and elevated to knighthood, hence the "Sir" thereafter before his name. In 1523 he was assigned as Speaker of the House of Commons, a significant occurrence because More instigated immunity for all members for remarks made in the Commons, a constitutional guarantee and landmark that continues today. Shortly, he was made High Steward over both Oxford and Cambridge Universities and received further benefices especially the lucrative 1525 Vice-Chancellorship of the Duchy of Lancaster. All of these appointments were based on his service to King and court. In 1524 More moved his family out of London to a farmhouse along the Thames River in Chelsea and began to build his new home and estate. He borrowed considerable funds from the King for the project, a thirty-four acre estate centered by what he called his 'greatest house', More's own term for his family's largest house ever.

War also raged throughout this decade of the 1520's—England v. France; Holy Roman Emperor/King of Spain v. Rome and the Pope, etc. Alliances came and went, dynastic and religious issues playing roles. As the decade neared end in

1529, three major forces were faced by the new Lord Chancellor of England-war, Reformation, and the King's 'great matter.'

VIII

"When a man takes an oath, Meg, he's holding his own self in his own hands, like water. And if he opens his fingers then he needn't hope to find himself again."

> **Robert Bolt, A Man For All Seasons. Quoted by House of Representatives Judiciary Committee Chairman, Henry J. Hyde, before the United States Senate, January 14, 1999, opening the Trial of President William J. Clinton.**

Thomas More never enjoyed court life. Henry VIII regularly teased him about his feelings, never considering him the less valuable to his needs, however. More's reputation as a scholar, author, and diplomat found him held in high respect on the continent. As Henry's annulment issue developed the King saw More's standing a valuable aid across the English Channel, certainly a factor in the King elevating him to the Chancellorship. The

King spoke to More again about his 'great matter' immediately after More's appointment in 1529. Perhaps Henry believed being made the second most powerful man in the realm would bring More to reverse his position and accept that the marriage was invalid. He also sent the Archbishops of Canterbury and of York, England's second largest city at the time, to influence him. He badly wanted More to be a member of the pro-annulment team, whose membership was swelling. But More did not waver from his earlier view of the marriage's validity. As Peter Ackroyd states he "believed the original papal dispensation to have been valid and the marriage (to Catherine) sound." More never again spoke to anyone, including his wife and family, of his words to the King. Neither would he ever advise anyone how to form his or her conscience, arrive at his or her own decision on the annulment issue, or on the matter of oaths later required of them. Clearly as Thomas More became Lord Chancellor his mind and conscience were set on the 'great matter' and he would soon be on a collision course with his King and with the course of history.

The dynastic wars of Europe quieted after 1529. Thomas More had aided in this with his diplomatic efforts in establishing the Peace Leagues at

Cambrai. Elsewhere in Europe, however, the invading Turkish forces of Suleiman the Magnificent were a serious threat to Christianity as they neared Vienna and occupied parts of Eastern Europe. Chancellor More focused on the 'unity' of the Church both internally and externally. Growing support for the King's side in the 'great matter', however, and More's refusal to discuss it, increasingly isolated him. Church hierarchy, parliament, and the Court joined the King's cause.

IX

"...we receive from that See (Rome) our crown Imperial."

Henry VIII in 1521

In 1532 Henry gained a major victory when the parliament enacted his law known as "the submission of the clergy." All ecclesiastical laws now were subject to his approval. The day after this law's enactment, Thomas More was allowed to resign as Lord Chancellor. He had much earlier asked the Duke of Norfolk to intercede with the King to allow him to retire. In 1530 More had developed a chest pain and he used this as a reason to step down. Court physicians warned him the malady could be serious. No doubt Henry kept Thomas More as Chancellor until the clergy issue was passed by parliament, giving the appearance that More was in agreement. Henry VIII met him in the York Place garden in Westminster on Thursday, May 16, 1532 at 3 p.m. and accepted the Great Seal of office from his long time servant and advisor. The two men never saw one another or communicated directly again.

Events moved rapidly after More turned over the Great Seal. Anxious to expedite his annulment, Henry sent a commission to the Pope. Ill timed and poorly staffed, including among others Anne Boleyn's father, it was unsuccessful. An appeal to approve annulment was sent by the peerage and Church prelates to the Pope. Neither Thomas More nor Bishop John Fisher signed it, an omission that almost caused the King to remove More as Chancellor then. This petition, too, went unanswered. Then, in February of 1533 Henry secretly married Anne Boleyn, now one month with child - the future Elizabeth I. Thomas Cromwell and Archbishop of Canterbury Thomas Cranmer moved to legally invalidate Catherine as Queen. In April, 1533 Anne Boleyn was coronated Queen in Westminster Abbey. Still no decision had come from Rome. Finally, on July 1, 1533 Pope Clement VII acted, excommunicating Henry and declaring his marriage to Anne Boleyn invalid. It was then almost another year on March 23, 1534 that he announced the marriage of Henry and Catherine to be valid, a matter that had been unanswered for seven years. The Papacy was near the nadir of its prestige in the 1520's following its decline during the Renaissance Age, the threat of Turkish invasion from the east, the political domination and sacking of Rome by the Holy Roman Emperor, the spread of the Reformation and the immorality of many popes. If events made Pope Clement VII indecisive, Henry VIII was willful and determined to achieve his goal, defined in 1533 as absolute control over the Church in England. Henry's status with his people and the low standing of the See of Rome produced only one Bishop, John Fisher, and one layman, Thomas More, along with a small number of clergy who would subsequently refuse allegiance to the oath required of all to approve the King's elevation as "Protector and Supreme Head of the Church in England."

In early 1534 More wrote Thomas Cromwell, the person of most influence in the court and the liaison to the King, a final letter. It recalled King Henry's stance on the matter of papal primacy in 1521. More added that the 15th century Council of Florence had stated that the Bishop of Rome "in blessed Peter there was given over by our Lord Jesus Christ full power to pasture, to rule, to govern the whole church." More also lauded a recent interest of the King's in supporting a call for a General Council "for in the next general council it may well happen that this Pope may be deposed and another substituted in his room with whom the King's Highness may be very well content." He continued "never thought I the Pope above the general council nor have in any book of mine put forth among the King's subjects in our vulgar tongue, advanced greatly the Pope's authority." But nowhere in this letter does More approve a ruler or nation deciding any matter contrary to the policy of pope or general council. E.E. Reynold's <u>St. Thomas More</u> attests to More's English writings and views expressed in that letter. Further, Thomas More sent this letter for the King to hear or read as he had asked Norfolk to intercede with the King to allow his earlier resignation and Norfolk and Wolsey to intercede and improve his difficult financial status in the past. More never spoke directly to the monarch about his own personal matters or beliefs. Only when asked did he reply, otherwise he accepted 'the royal will'. Here in the Cromwell letter More was urging patience and alignment with the decision of a future Pope or council, a plea to keep England within the Church.

But Henry awaited no new pope, no general council. He would near the end of his reign when the Council of Trent finally met in 1545 to address reform and inaugurate the Catholic Reformation. Whether More's letter, affirming his continuing commitment to Christian unity, triggered his treatment at Lambeth Palace and in the Tower soon after, we can not say. Certainly, by April of 1534, King Henry knew his long time advisor and servant had steadfastly stood against his annulment cause, his marriage to Anne Boleyn, her coronation, and his expanding policy to end all influence of the See of Rome in England. More was also seen as 'tainted' by a perception of allegiance to Catherine, the 'Dowager Queen'. But he had never conspired with her or her followers though she admired him above all Henry's courtiers and servants. He also came under suspicion for perceived support for Elizabeth Barton, the 'sad Nun of Kent', whose prophecies about events, including the danger of Henry and Anne's relationship, developed a cult following. More, like Henry himself, met the woman but never denounced her until her public recantation of her visions at St. Paul's Cross in late 1533. More then called her "a false deceiving hypocrite." But his loyalty to Henry was under added suspicion.

X

"I pray thee, Mistress Alice, tell me one thing. Is not this house as nigh heaven as my own?"

Thomas More replies to his wife after her caustic criticism of his life in the Tower cell room.

When Thomas More left the role of Lord Chancellor, he returned to live full time at his Chelsea estate. Knowing his income would quickly decline, he sold off the family's gold and silver plate for about four hundred pounds, a significant sum at the time. Assembling his family he presented the financial realities ahead and asked for comments. When none came, he lectured them in a memorable speech on their need to contribute more and prepare to accept a simpler fare and style of life at 'the greatest house'. In truth his wife and children were protected financially and owned property as well. His goal was to prepare them for an uncertain future and possible enmity of the King and his advisors. More also reduced his staff and employees but charitably placed every person with another employer. Henry Patenson, the family 'fool' and servant who appears in one of the Holbein family portraits, was placed with the Mayor of London. On his estate More had a small house near the Thames and the Chelsea Church where he went for privacy, prayer, meditation and self-mortification. He gave this house with about seven acres, called Butclose, to Will and Meg Roper for their family, ensuring they would not lose it in case an attainder was passed against him in the future. Dame Alice appeared very distressed at her husband's action and its consequences. She seems to have blamed him for his resignation and later imprisonment. We have only two recorded conversations between them. The first occurred in Chelsea parish church where More found her after his resignation as Chancellor. She was stunned at what he had done and extremely upset. Later, in the presence of Margaret she castigated her husband in his cell in the Tower for choosing "to lie here in this close, filthy prison, and be content thus to be shut up amongst mice and rats, when you might be abroad at your liberty, and with the favour and good will of the King and his Council, if you would but do as all Bishops and best learned of this realm have done." More's ever gentle response to his wife was to say the cell was as close to heaven as was his own house. Our knowledge of Alice is limited as she certainly destroyed letters and some papers to protect the family from future searches. She had inherited wealth and property but felt embarrassment and disgrace from her husband's alienation from the King. Thomas More had made efforts to protect and financially provide for his wife and other family members, however.

He continued to write in the vernacular mainly against the heresy of 'reform', which was moving closer to the King. Henry believed himself, his views, his policies to be wholly 'Catholic' until the day he died. He regularly attended mass, viewing himself as the valid 'defender of the faith'. Those close to the King were cautious, less they be seen as tainted by heresy. Following the Nun of Kent affair a bill was drawn naming Thomas More in support of a plot against the King. He was brought to testify but in a significant defense, succeeded in having his name removed before parliament considered the legislation. More told Roper: "I have given the Devil a foul fall." He knew, too, he was preparing for possible future 'oaths' of loyalty. In April of 1533 he antagonized Henry by declining an invitation to attend the coronation of Queen Anne in Westminster. Several Bishops invited him and sent funds with which to buy suitable attire. More kept the twenty pounds, remarking : "I need it more than you do..." while refusing to attend. Two years later at his trial More's final words were that his was no crime of treason but that :"I know full well what has been the cause of my condemnation: it is that I would never give my approval to this new marriage."

On April 12, 1534 after attending a Palm Sunday lecture at St. Paul's, More was given a summons to appear at Lambeth Palace the following morning. He knew 'oaths' were about to be required . On Monday after being confessed and Mass he bade his family farewell and, accompanied by Roper, went down the Thames to the Archbishop's Palace. En route he happily said: "Son Roper, I thank our Lord, the field is won." Roper believed his father-in-law was expressing that "love of God wrought in him so effectively that it conquered his carnal affections utterly." But More had a different meaning to his words. Upon earlier bidding his family farewell, Thomas More had symbolically closed the fence separating his property from the Thames embankment, placing himself apart from them. He knew his 'wait' was over, the final act was beginning and he had to keep his mind and conscience clear and focused.

He had revealed to no one the reasons his conscience was fixed. Rather than Roper's idea of carnal control, More had a deeper conviction to his words. Knowing the sadness of possibly never seeing family members again, he took strength from the purity his soul could achieve and his determination neither to falter by swearing to what his conscience did not confirm, nor to reveal his reasons for remaining silent. Examination at Lambeth Palace would lead to imprisonment in the Tower but he was confident.

XI

"My son, Roper, the field is won."

Thomas More en route to Lambeth Palace and the Tower of London.

Four of Henry VIII's foremost advisers met Thomas More that April 13, 1534-Archbishop of Canterbury Thomas Cranmer, Lord Chancellor Thomas Audley, Principal Secretary to the King Thomas Cromwell and the Abbot of Westminster William Benson. The Act of Succession passed by Parliament in early 1533 did several things: invalidated Henry's marriage to Catherine, validated his marriage to Anne with their children becoming heirs to the throne, and rejected any Papal authority in matters of marriage in England. It also called for an 'oath' to be required under penalty of imprisonment and loss of goods. This continued the transfer of papal power and authority in England to the King, a process begun in 1533 with the submission of the clergy, royal appointment of Bishops and other church hierarchy, and royal control over monasteries with their considerable wealth. By 1536 Henry would replace the Pope in all areas of authority and control over matters of the Church in England. The four men who met Thomas More provided him a copy of the new Act of Succession and an 'oath' to the act for him to sign. The 'oath' went beyond the terms of the Act, which did not go into force for another month on May 1, and was not in full agreement with it. More viewed it as an illegal document. Further, he could not and would not, in conscience, perjure himself by signing it. Parliament had not authorized this 'oath', which extended the King's power above any "foreign authority, Prince or Potentate", clearly meaning the Pope, in all matters. More was not moved by his interrogators' attempts to frighten him with danger of the King's "great indignation" if he did not sign. He was given four days to change his mind. Kept in the monastery at Westminster, More refused again to take the 'oath', giving no reason he would not. More then was imprisoned in the Tower of London, the only lay person so committed over this 'great matter'. Bishop John Fisher went for similar reasons, as did five priests including the prominent Dr. Nicholas Wilson. No other church hierarchy refused the 'oath' and in time only a small number of clergy joined More and Fisher.

Thomas More knew the Lambeth Commission would send him to the Tower. Of the others similarly imprisoned, Dr. Wilson and two of the clergy would recant and take the oath and be released. The other two priests were held in the Tower until executed in 1540. Bishop Fisher, imprisoned in the second floor Bell Tower room, and More in the cell room immediately below were forever connected - the lone Bishop and the sole layman to reject the 'oath', and to suffer martyrdom within weeks of each other in 1535.Four hundred years later Pope Pius XI canonized them as Saints. In 1535 Thomas More was fifty seven years of age, John Fisher was seventy six.

When More closed the gate on his Chelsea estate, leaving his family behind, he did not know if execution lay ahead but believed he would never be free. To take the 'oath' was to violate his conscience, an act of perjury - the turning away from God who was party to the taking of an oath. To commit perjury was to lose his soul and never achieve heaven. More would have sworn an 'oath' on the sole matter of succession to the throne for he, like Fisher, agreed that that decision was one the monarch and parliament had the right to decide. But the 'oath' given him at Lambeth went beyond succession and required allegiance to the exclusion of the Pope, the See of Rome, from matters of marriage and religious decisions in England. To this More would never ascent. His being 'silent' on his reason for rejecting the 'oath' was primary to More as well. To give his reason would provide evidence against him, supporting a charge of treason. He knew he was innocent of treason and, thus, had to stay 'silent'. Further, he wrote "in common law and in natural justice a man can not be found guilty for his thoughts" and these he kept to himself until after he was found guilty at Trial on July 1, 1535. Thomas More believed he was imprisoned unjustly and died in the firm belief he had never committed treason.

Throughout More's Tower months Henry VIII tried unsuccessfully to break his will. He used others - Dame Alice, Margaret among them, to pressure his prisoner. On November 3,1534 the Reformation Parliament reconvened and proceeded to pass three acts affecting More directly. The Act of Supremacy proclaimed Henry as "the only supreme head on earth of the Church in England, called *Anglica Ecclesia*", thus creating the Anglican Church. A treason act followed making for the first time a capital offence to "maliciously wish, will, or desire, by words or writing to deprive the royal family of dignity, title and such or to declare the King erratic, schismatic, tyrant or infidel." And, finally, Parliament passed two acts of attainder, one against Fisher and the imprisoned clergy, the other solely against Thomas More for "intending to sow sedition" by refusing the 'oath' of succession and of having ungratefully served his sovereign lord, the King. This act forfeited More's lands and goods to the Crown, which were later given in large part to members and friends of Queen Anne's family. Is it any wonder that Thomas More and his family saw his opposition to the marriage of Anne Boleyn to Henry VIII as the real reason for his imprisonment and execution?

Other changes occurred once these acts were passed. Until late 1534 More was allowed occasional visitors, some freedom on the Tower grounds and attendance at mass in the two Tower chapels. These liberties ceased once treason and capital punishment became law. Dame Alice made the one known visit in 1534 and most likely came again just before his execution. Daughter Margaret, pregnant with a son to be named Thomas, was her father's confidant, correspondent and visitor. Initially she tried to influence her father to take the 'oath'. All of More's family took the oath, though Margaret, at least, included the exception "as far as would stand with the law of God." Her father was deeply hurt by Margaret's attempt to influence his conscience. Without giving her specific reason, he replied to her "lamentable letter which in such inherent piteous manner labor to dissuade unto me, that thing I have of pure necessity for respect unto mine own soul, so often given you so precise answer before." The matter was not pursued though Margaret, and all her family, remained ever hopeful he would one day be released.

Henry and Cromwell used Margaret in 1535, hopeful to influence her father. Five more priests, three Carthusian priors and two others, all well known to Thomas More, refused the 'oath' and were imprisoned in the Tower in April. They were quickly tried and convicted under the new Act of Treason. Cromwell, who had interrogated More on April 30, accused him of influencing other men, presumably referring to the five religious just convicted. He also promised More the King wished to release him if he took the 'oath'. But More again refused, replying : "I do no harm, I say none harm, I think none harm, but wish everybody good. And if this be not enough to keep a man alive, in good faith I long not to live." A few days later Margaret was allowed to visit. It was May 4, the day the priors - one from the London Charterhouse, and the two other priests were tied to bundles and dragged off from the Tower to terrible torture and death at Tyburn. Meg and her father saw them leave, watching from a small, narrow slit in his cell, listening to their joyous singing as they went to be with Christ. More lifted his daughter's spirit, seeing them like happy bride grooms at their wedding. He extolled their joyous martyrdom and expressed his envy that they would shortly be in heaven. The King and his men hoped Meg's visit would influence More on this fearful day but in fact his resolve turned even stronger.

XII

the "prayers of the Saint are the best mirrors of his mind and soul."

Abbe' Germain Marc'hadour in Praying with Saint Thomas More.

Praying was a constant, ceaseless aspect of Thomas More's life. He wrote, copied and memorized countless prayers, required extensive daily prayer by his family and himself. Regular prayer, meditation, and flagellation had their origins with Jesus and the early Church and his practice of these three disciplines speaks to the core of the man. His letters always included prayerful words, ending frequently with the phrase 'your bedeman', binding him to pray for the recipient. In the Tower his Psalter, prayer books and other materials had their margins filled with his prayers, notes and meditations. He regularly said: "Give me thy grace, good Lord...to think my most enemies my best friends." Following the Jesus Psalter, he prayed ten times each day for a straighter road to heaven by asking :"Send me here my purgatory." Late in his Tower experience he told Margaret he was indebted to King Henry for his imprisonment for it had deepened his spiritual life.

More's Tower writings and recorded conversations were related indirectly to the defense of his conscience, as he tried to explain to family and friends why he had to take the stand he did. "He had to do so", says Anne Murphy, "in a way that was discreet, so that nothing he said or wrote could be construed against him in court. In the privacy of his prayer and meditation he had to discern whether he was taking the right action or not. This 'outer' dialogue, with friends, and 'inner' dialogue, with God and his conscience, pursued within a strategy of legal prudence and hardheadedness, constituted the core of his prison experience. His prison writings in defense of conscience, in preparation for death, are among the finest in the whole Christian tradition."

The Tower writings include his letters - thirteen have been preserved; A Dialogue of Comfort Against Tribulation; On the Sadness, Weariness, Fear and Prayer of Christ before His Passion (in Latin); and a small work on receiving the Blessed Body of Our Lord. Conscience is a big component of his existing letters, More believing each person responsible only to God to ensure the 'inner' conscience agrees with one's actions, the 'outer' conscience. The soul is the 'eye of the heart' and must agree with the will of God. Anything else endangers the loss of heaven. Eight of these letters went to Margaret and were for all Sir Thomas' family with messages for Lady Alice and specific children.

A lengthy, occasionally rambling work, Dialogue of Comfort was written on many levels. Set in Hungary, beset by the Ottoman invasion of the time, its two primary characters represent strength (comfort) and weakness (tribulation) as well as good and evil, unity and division, and other themes. Meant to convey his own inner decisions to family, he referenced the Bible, Christian writers and themes, and a number of topics relating to the age and to imprisonment, martyrdom, heresy, torture, fear, and, most frequently, suicide. Dialogue of Comfort held that acts of faith, hope and charity lead to the conquest of God's love and salvation.

The shorter Sadness of Christ was written in the months immediately before his death. As in all Tower writings it helped focus on his own needs, his own approaching martyrdom, his own soul's safe passage to heaven. Written in Latin for an educated audience, it focused on Christ at Gethsemane, his isolation, his human fear, his martyrdom and his example. He had previously written on the Passion of Christ but in the Tower his meditation and authorship had a new urgency.

XIII

"Not Guilty!"

Like More, Bishop John Fisher faced repeated interrogations to extract his 'oath' to Henry's Acts but he, too, refused. In Rome in late May of 1535 Paul III succeeded Clement VII. The new Pope believed he could have Bishop Fisher released from prison in England if he made him a Cardinal, requiring him to come to Rome. Instead, upon hearing of Fisher's elevation, Henry VIII was furious, and announced he would send Fisher's head to Rome for the red hat of a Cardinal. He also ordered Fisher and More immediately take the 'oath' testifying to him as Head of the Church in England. Neither would do so. Henry then ordered they be preached against in all churches for having committed treason. On June 3 More was interrogated by Cromwell, Cranmer, Audley and the Queen's father and brother. The Boleyn family had become a major player in the affair. On June 12 John Fisher, now stripped of his ecclesiastical title by the King, had his last interrogation. On the same day More's cell was stripped by two of Cromwell's servants of all books and writing materials. With them came Richard Rich, the Solicitor General, who engaged More in conversation. Later, at More's trial Rich would testify that Thomas More had committed an act of treason. Back in May Rich had tricked John Fisher into denying Henry's supremacy. But More never spoke the words Rich later alleged.

On June 12 Bishop John Fisher was tried at Westminster for treason, found guilty and condemned to death at Tyburn. The morning of June 17, 1535 it was decided he was too frail to sustain the five mile dragging to the torture and death at Tyburn, site of the present Marble Arch, and his sentence was changed to beheading on nearby Tower Hill. After joyfully going to his execution, Fisher's head was placed on a pole atop London Bridge until, becoming comely and attracting large crowds, it was ordered to be thrown into the Thames. His body was buried in All Hollow's Church but, again, crowds came in a sort of pilgrimage and it was reburied in St. Peter ad Vincula.

When another interrogation in June proved futile, Thomas More was placed on trial on July 1, 1535. As was the custom, he was alone, with no witnesses, no lawyer, no aid of any kind. He did not know the indictment with its four counts until he was brought into King's Bench at Westminster, the very room in which his father had served as Judge. More's jury was composed of nineteen jurors, thirteen of whom served on Fisher's jury, and included his former interrogators and other nobility and high officials. Queen Anne's father, brother and uncle were jurors. Lord Chancellor Thomas Audley conducted the trial. No member of the More family was allowed to attend the trial, though his three sons-in-law sat in the House of Commons.

Thomas More suffered physically during his Tower months. Since 1530 he had a chronic chest pain, court physicians told him was serious. He suffered severe leg cramps and experienced 'gravel and stone', kidney stone attack, so painful he thought he would die. At his trial he was gaunt and weak for he ate but one meal a day usually meat, and had to walk with a staff and sit in a chair. But his mind was clear. He heard the indictment of treason and the four specific counts. He pleaded : "Not Guilty!" He knew he had not deprived the King of his title as head of the Church of England. Three of the four counts referred to his silence and collusions with a convicted traitor, John Fisher.

More easily defended himself against all three counts. The final count charged on June 12 he spoke to Sir Richard Rich in his cell against Parliament's right to make Henry head of the Church of England. So it came down to Rich's word against More's. Thomas More's attack on Rich, whom he had long known, and on the absurdity to believe that he, who had so long kept silent to all men, would reveal his view to one like Rich, was devastating. Rich then called the two servants ,present packing More's items on June 12, to testify they heard what Rich alleged. But neither man could do so. More was not guilty and all present must have known it. But the King wished Thomas More to die, as did the Queen. And the nineteen man jury voted him guilty.

Thomas More then spoke, breaking his silence at last. He charged the indictment was illegal by God's law. He denied any right to pass an act repugnant to the spiritual rule of the Catholic Church and the See of Rome, denying England could act outside 'Christ's Universal Church'. Biographer Peter Ackroyd provides his final words:... "That though your Lordships have now here in the earth been judges to my condemnation, we may yet hereafter merrily all meet together, to our everlasting salvation and thus I desire

Almighty God to preserve and defend the King's Majesty, and to send him good counsel." Amazing words from a condemned man! All that was left was for Lord Chancellor Audley to read aloud the sentence of death at Tyburn: "Sir Thomas More, you are to be drawn on a hurdle through the City of London to Tyburn, there to be hanged till you be half dead, after that cut down yet alive, your bowels to be taken out of your body and burned before you, your privy parts cut off, your head cut off, your body divided in four parts, and your head and body to be set at such places as the King shall assign."

XIV

"...it is a case in which a man may lose his head and yet have none harm."

St. Thomas More before his execution

Returning under guard from Westminster to the Tower , Thomas More knew he was innocent, feeling none of the disgrace attached to conviction of high treason. He had defended himself, firm in his belief that divine law was superior to human law. Unperturbed, charitable and loyal he had been prepared for the trial he knew he would not win and was now ready for the fearful torture and death it meant. Some family members awaited him near the Tower. His son John knelt and, weeping, asked for his father's blessing, a loving act recalling to Sir Thomas his own prior relation to his father before whom he had regularly knelt for a blessing even when Lord Chancellor. Beloved Margaret twice threw herself upon him, fearless of the guards, to kiss her father and openly express her love and respect. These acts moved More deeply as he wrote in his last letter to his family, written in coal on an algarism stone which was picked up by Dorothy Cooley, Meg's maid, the day before his execution. This July 5 letter to his dear ones contained thirty six lines, used the verb 'pray' eleven times, and the epitaph 'good' fifteen times. It included his memorable saying that "nothing can come but that God wills." The omission of any mention of his wife meant Lady Alice had certainly been written separately or, more likely, as was the custom, had been allowed a private final visit with her husband. More's love and affection for his wife was evident in his Tower days, attested to by his words in letters to Meg. Lady Alice had written both King Henry VIII and Thomas Cromwell early in 1535 to appeal for her husband's release but to no avail. At his death she was certainly feeling some measure of anger towards him for the disgrace, danger and financial difficulty his actions had meant to her and the family.

In the days after the trial, one of the most famous in English history, King Henry changed the execution from torture at Tyburn to beheading on Tower Hill. Many writers have stated the reason as the King's remembrance of earlier affection and high regard for Thomas More. But other factors were surely involved. John Fisher's execution had been changed to Tower Hill because of his frailty. Thomas More, needing a staff to walk, was gaunt, gray, drained by the infirmities of his body of which the Crown knew, and weak from fasting. He, too, might not endure the five mile dragging through London's cobblestone streets to Tyburn. Of greater significance in altering his sentence was the King's concern for public approval. More had served London and its people well and was in high regard there. Fisher, a humanist scholar and man of piety, was known for his devotion to the city's poor and needy. Crowds had turned out under his head exhibited atop London Bridge and before his body's burial site. The King was wary of other such venerations and the start of a cult in adoration. By executing More on Tower Hill, Henry lessened the crowd size, controlled the short route from cell to execution place and minimized possible public displeasure. To further condemn More, searches of his Chelsea estate, including Butclose where the Ropers now lived, were conducted, hopeful of discovering incriminating materials. None were unearthed, however, to justify the treason charge further. After More's death this form of suspicion and searching continued and the More family lived under apprehension for decades. Henry also feared foreign reaction for Thomas More was in high standing among rulers and the erudite of the continent. It was to Henry's advantage to execute More in a fashion viewed to be more humane.

XV

"I am the King's good servant but God's first."

St. Thomas More on the Tower Hill scaffold, July 6, 1535.

Believing the body to be but "the garment of the soul", Thomas More was devoted to the control of this covering, using Jesus' Passion as his model. His final days were spent on prayer and meditation, often in the prone position, reminiscent of Jesus at Gethsemane. He fasted, probably slept little if at all. He refused a barber sent to cut his hair and long beard. Surely, news of the change in his execution method lessened the human fear, making it easier "to walk the narrow way" and "to enter by the strait gate to heaven." Easier, too, to keep a narrow focus for the 'eye of his heart'- his soul, and have his conscience ever conform to the Will of God. His only wish was "to go to God" on July 6, a Feast Day of St. Thomas a' Beckett also martyred for defying a King named Henry, and beloved since childhood by More.

Early on Tuesday, July 6, Sir Thomas Pope, Warden of the Royal Mint inside the Tower walls, informed Thomas More he would be executed at nine a.m. that day. Pope, like the Constable of the Tower, Sir William Kingston, held More in the highest regard. More had to console each of these men during these last days. For himself he welcomed the news. He wore a worn cloak of John a' Wood's, and carried a red cross. He arranged for a gold coin, an 'angel', for his executioner. If the cloak was the symbol of a 'common man', the red cross signified his knighthood and the Passion of Jesus Christ. He lived out his own words, written twenty years earlier in Utopia, that "no part of his life is more frequently or more gladly spoken of than his cheerful death."

At nine o'clock Thomas More passed through the middle Tower and along the west side of the Tower of London's outer walls. He was openly cheerful and merry. He may have spoken and jested with members of the gathered crowd. On the King's orders no family were present. Margaret Clement, wife of More's protégé, John Clement, was present, representing the More family. Once outside the walls his escort was assumed by a sheriff of London, Humphrey Monmouth, who had once been imprisoned in the Tower for heretical views by More. On Tower Hill's rickety scaffold stairs, officers supported him, causing him to remark :"...when I come down again let me shift for myself as well as I can." As John Fisher had sung the 'Te Deum' on the scaffold, More prayed the 'Miserere'. Dutiful to the last, he kept his remarks brief. Warden Pope had earlier conveyed to him the "King's pleasure ...that at your execution you shall not use many words." More had promised to "readily obediently to confirm myself to his grace's commandments." On the scaffold he told the large assemblage to pray for him as he would for them and asked they pray for the King "that it might please God to give him good counsel." He concluded that he was "the King's good servant but God's first."

Thomas More then blessed and kissed his executioner, urging him to "pluck up thy spirit...my neck is short...strike away..." Covering his face with a linen cloth, stretching his beard, then his arms, before him, Thomas More placed his head on the block. He died with a single blow of the axe.

The body of Thomas More was taken to St. Peter ad Vincula, a Tower chapel. His daughter Meg and her maid performed the sad duty of wrapping his body in a cloth for burial. Historian

Thomas Macauley later spoke of this place :"There is no sadder spot on earth than this little cemetery." John Fisher's body was shortly reburied here, too. Par boiled and placed on a pole atop London Bridge, More's head after some weeks was given to Meg Roper who had bribed the executioner for it.

XVI

St. Thomas More, that "perfectly balanced man."

Pope Pius XI at the martyr's canonization, May 19, 1935.

And so began the martyrdom of Roman Catholics in England. The faith did not expire but stayed alive through faithful believers, sustained by the memory of men like Thomas More, John Fisher and hundreds of other martyrs. Numerous priests, some one hundred and sixty alone ordained in France at Allen Hall, would suffer death in England in the years after 1535. By 1886 the Papacy under Leo XIII decided to beatify fifty-four of these early martyrs, headed by Thomas More and John Fisher. In the twentieth century appeals arose for canonization, including from members of the legal profession who had adopted More as a model. The elevation of John Cardinal Fisher and Thomas More to Sainthood occurred in 1935 on the four hundredth anniversary of their martyrdoms. Alone among saints the two had no miracles attributed to them. It was the unquestioned splendor of their lives and of their deaths that warranted their joint elevations.

Capable of prophetic insights, St. Thomas More did not foresee the spread of his ideas, his values, his example, and his very name. The Thomas More Societies of North America organize and advance his views to lawyers and others. Near the Potomac River on Capital Hill in Washington, D.C., their statue of him is meant to inspire judges, legislators, and all citizens who visit the Church of St. Joseph. Elsewhere, across the English speaking world, churches, schools, colleges, universities bear his name. Many More family and friends migrated after his death to France and the *'Amici Thomae Mori'*, begun in 1962 sustains his memory and values through its splendid publications, conferences and great influence. The Thomas More Society of London was begun by an Irishman from Cork to organize lawyers of the world for More's canonization and continues today. The Saint would be humbled and suprised that in America, on a continent almost unknown in his era, private Yale University collected, edited and published all his known writings, some fifteen volumes, and support a world renowned center that continues study of his life and works. Numerous biographies and monographs have resulted.

The Saint's example helped Catholicism survive in England, while the two religions he opposed, Anglicanism and Lutheranism, grew and expanded after his death. Anne Murphy observes: "More actually had most in common with those whom he implaccably opposed: religious leaders like Luther and Tynsdale who were motivated by a genuine desire to preach the gospel." And E.E. Reynold's in St. Thomas More finds an interesting shift in More in his Tower work, Dialogue of Comfort, when he seeks common ground with the Lutheran doctrine of justification by faith. More wrote: "Thereof will I let God work and leave off contention; and nothing shall I now say, but that with which they that are themselves of the contrary mind shall in reason have no cause to be discontented." More's Prayer Book had more notes on the Psalm devoted to unanimity in the house of God than on any other Old Testament verse. His own life of prayer was always connected with the unity of the universal Church. He took this view to his prison meditation, away from the political life of court and King.

XVII

"Give me thy Grace, good Lord,
To set the world at nought,
To set my mind fast upon Thee..."

St. Thomas More's Tower prayer.

Today St. Thomas More would see hope for a return of unity. On October 31, 1999 an historic agreement was signed in Augsburg, Germany on the doctrine of justification and faith the very issue that triggered the Protestant Reformation. For three decades the Vatican and Pope John Paul II and the Lutheran World Federation have met and dialogued on this issue, signing the joint Declaration on the Doctrine of Justification on a date and in a city commemorative of Martin Luther's founding beliefs of over four hundred years ago.

St. Thomas would also be merry to know of the forty three page document, "A Gift of Authority", issued in London's Westminster Abbey by Anglican Archbishop of Canterbury Reverend

George Carey, urging the world's seventy million Anglicans to read its "Recognition of the place of the pope in the church's family." The product of an Anglican and Roman Catholic International Commission begun in 1966, it was issued in the Spring of 1999. In the year 2000 a millennium meeting will be held in Canada of Anglican and Catholic archbishops to discuss healing their four century rift begun in 1534. Quietly, too, recent years have seen clergy of the religions changing church allegiances. In England some four hundred Anglican ministers have become Catholic priests, while some thirty Catholic clergy have become ministers. In the United States one hundred Episcopalian priests and some Lutheran ministers have entered the Catholic Church as priests.

G.K. Chesterton, himself a convert to Catholicism in England, prophecized in 1936 that "Thomas More is more important at this moment than at any moment since his death ...but he is not quite as important as he will be in a hundred year's time. He may come to be counted the greatest Englishman, or at least the greatest historical character in English history."

In London Monsignor Anthony Stark of the Guild of Our Lady of Ransom prepares for another day long pilgrimage in early July to study and venerate St. Thomas More. The annual, ever more popular, journey begins in Chelsea, boats down the Thames to the City and the martyr's cell in the Tower, ending with Mass on Tower Hill. During this millennium year the Anglican Church is honoring Thomas More along the Thames River. The Catholic Church celebrates Jubilee 2000 announced by the Bishop of Rome, Pope John Paul II. Saint Thomas More is surely praying for a millennium of Christian unity, knowing well that "nothing can come but that which God wills." His own example would place charity and peace atop the priorities of the world's statesmen and politicians, who would also be shown how to not take themselves too seriously.

Notes...

1. Margaret Roper placed her father's head in a small lead casket after receiving it from the executioner she had bribed for it. Upon her death in 1544 it passed to her daughter, then to William Roper. Though Roper's will called for him to be buried in the More Vault of the Chelsea Old Church by his wife, he was placed in the Roper Vault in St. Dunstan's Church, Canterbury. It is here that the decomposed head of Thomas More in its casket was found in the 1980's excavation. The Church has a video of More's life and of the present status of his head, narrated by Anglican Pastor Maurice Worgan. Both of More's wives were buried in the More Vault at Chelsea.

2. The hairshirt Thomas More wore is in the possession of the Cannonesses Regular of Newton Abbot. A piece of the relic is at The Church of the Most Holy Redeemer and St. Thomas More in Chelsea. The metal box used to transport it on July 5, 1535 from the Tower cell is on display in the small parlor room of Allen Hall, Beaufort Street, Chelsea, London.

Allen Hall is the current seminary and study center for the Roman Catholic Archdiocese of Westminster (London). It is on the site of More's "greatest house"; a mulberry tree and part of a Tudor brick wall from the era are still visible.

3. Abbe' Germain Marc' hadour and Jocelyne Malhomme tell us in Praying with Saint Thomas More that "More's cruellest ordeal was not to be shut up in the 'strait room' of his prison cell (he had practiced and welcomed that kind of solitude) but for him, the companionable commoner, to look odd and 'singular' in his opposition to the will of his 'natural lord', the King. He also confesses to Meg his yearning to 'talk with my friends, and especially my wife and you that pertain to my charge'." That his family and friends could not know his reasons, understand his silence, was his greatest purgatory.

4. Lady Alice More resented, too, the 15 shilling weekly charge to her for Tower food and keep for her husband and his man servant, John a' Wood. She was absent outside the Tower after the Trial with the children and at his burial in St. Peter ad Vincula. Her first husband, John Middleton, was buried only four hundred yards

away in St. Katherine's Coleman Cemetery, possibly making her attendance difficult. Or she may have become estranged from her husband's children. She did engage in a law suit with William Roper in later years over a matter of inheritance.

5. "Service to others", a hallmark of education in the Academy of Thomas More, continued with future descendants, many of whom became priests and nuns. The last known direct heir was Fr. Thomas More, S.J., the last head of the Jesuits in England before the Society's 18th century suppression.

6. At the canonization Pope Pius XI lauded the newest layman saint for his keenness of mind, his zeal for the salvation of souls and, perhaps chiefly, for "his bright example of Christian fortitude "In defending the faith even at the cost of his life. Forty seven years later, during his visit to Canterbury Cathedral with then Archbishop of Canterbury Robert Runcie, Pope John Paul II spoke of More's splendid example. Later, in a homily at London's Roman Catholic Westminster Cathedral, he used the occasion to honor Thomas More as "a fine scholar and an ornament to his profession, a loving husband and father, humble in prosperity, courageous in

adversity, humorous and godly" who died with Bishop John Fisher "victims of an unhappy age." The Pope asked his audience "to thank God for giving such men to England."

7. Canonized together on May 19, 1935, Saints Thomas More and John Fisher were placed on the universal church calendar in 1970, with a joint feast of June 22-the date of Fisher's execution.

8. The English Reformation during Henry's reign took other More friends and family. Giles Heron, husband of Cecily and Thomas More's son-in-law, was executed at Tyburn in 1540 as were priests close to More, including John Larke, pastor of the Chelsea Parish Church. Both son, John, and son-in-law, Will Roper, were imprisoned but released. Margaret Roper, too, was imprisoned briefly and interrogated over her keeping her father's head and letters. Her plea that she kept them, not to begin a cult but for her own loving memory of him, was believed and she was soon released.

9. William F. Buckley, Jr. in <u>Nearer My God : An Autobiograhy of Faith</u> compares More to another Christian martyr, stating that "Thomas

More Chapel and its well maintained kneelers. William Roper's circa 1550 Life of Sir Thomas More is a first hand and moving biography, used by all subsequent authors. Of course, More's own works are invaluable, though demanding. The publications, including regular periodicals, from *Amici Thomae Mori* are most valuable. I am told the recent Thomas More by J. McConica is provocative and thought provoking. Many other works could be cited. I hope this brief listing is useful.

11. South Korean President Kim Dae-Jung, who won the Nobel Peace Prize in 2000, experienced torture and imprisonment. A convert to Catholicism his Baptismal name was Thomas More.

12. The Martyr's cell in the Tower of London's Bell Tower is truly a haunting and moving place. A Tower Beefeater guides visitors and shows a short video and display on Thomas More's Life.

he front cover is a statue of "Sir Thomas ore" on Chelsea Embankment overlooking Thames River. On the rear of the statue in is printed "Saint." Chelsea Old Church More worshipped and where his two wives are buried in the More Vault, is visible to the rear. More holds the seal of Lord Chancellor.

About the author

C. Robert Wray holds the B.A. and M.A. in History from the University of Notre Dame. Following naval service he taught, coached and head-mastered for over three decades in independent schools. He and his wife currently live in North Falmouth on Cape Cod, Massachusetts and in Naples, Florida. They have four children and four grandchildren.

9 780759 604315